Reflections on Life

WHY WE'RE HERE
AND HOW TO ENJOY
THE JOURNEY

Compiled by Allen Klein

GRAMERCY BOOKS
NEW YORK

Published by Gramercy Books, an imprint of Random House Value Publishing, a division of Random House, Inc., New York.

Gramercy is a registered trademark and the colophon is a trademark of Random House, Inc.

Random House
New York • Toronto • London • Sydney • Auckland
www.randomhouse.com

Interior book design by Karen Ocker Design

Printed and bound in Singapore

A catalog record for this title is available from the Library of Congress.
ISBN-10: 0-517-22812-2
ISBN-13: 978-0-517-22812-8

10 9 8 7 6 5 4 3 2 1

*For my parents, who first gave me life,
and to all those who continue to enrich it.*

CONTENTS

INTRODUCTION

When I was a youngster, LIFE magazine was my television. Every Thursday afternoon, it brought the world to my mailbox. It showed me that there were ways of living that were very different from my fifth-floor-walkup Bronx existence. In addition, it showed me the commonalties, struggles, and celebrations of all people.

LIFE, the magazine, was also material for a bantering word game I played with my friends. We would repeatedly ask each other:

What's Life?
A magazine.
How much does it cost?
Twenty-five cents.
I only have a dime.
That's tough.
What's tough.
Life.
What's Life?
A magazine…

LIFE magazine suspended weekly publication many years ago, but the question of "What's life?" still is an intriguing one. Perhaps it is because there are so many answers to such a simple question; perhaps it is because none are right or wrong.

I was hoping that after collecting over 500 quotations that ponder this question, I might have a definitive answer of what life is. The best I could come up with at the end of my research, however, was that life was a magazine I used to read when I was growing up.

ALLEN KLEIN,
SAN FRANCISCO

**L'Chaim!
(To life!)**

JEWISH TOAST

What is life? We are born, we live a little and we die.

E. B. White, American writer

Getting born is like being given a ticket to the theatrical event called life. It's like going to the theater. Now, all that ticket will get you, is through the door. It doesn't get you a good time and it doesn't get you a bad time. You go in and sit down and you either love the show or you don't. If you do, terrific. And if you don't—that's show business.

Stewart Emery, *Actualizations*

What's life? I really don't know and that's OK. I can live with that. After all I don't know how my computer works and I still use that.

Rick Segel, author of *Retail Business Kit for Dummies*

The messiness of experience, that may be what we mean by life.

Daniel J. Boorstin, American writer

It is the "just this much" which is the millisecond after
millisecond of awareness and the "just this much" which
contains the enormity of Being found within being,
the sacred Presence that illuminates presence.

STEPHEN LEVINE, AUTHOR OF *WHO DIES?*

Life is a luminous halo, a semi-transparent envelope
surrounding us from the beginning.

VIRGINIA WOOLF, BRITISH NOVELIST

Life is the childhood of eternity.

JOHANN WOLFGANG VON GOETHE, GERMAN POET

One Life; a little gleam of Time between two Eternities.

THOMAS CARLYLE, *ON HEROES, HERO-WORSHIP, AND THE HEROIC IN HISTORY*

Life is a spell so exquisite that everything conspires to break it.

EMILY DICKINSON, AMERICAN POET

**The meaning of life lies in the oneness of all creation, which
combines supreme diversity with supreme interdependence.**

YEHUDI MENUHIN, BRITISH VIOLINIST

**Life is a process of becoming,
a combination of states we have to go through.**

ANAÏS NIN, FRENCH-BORN WRITER

**Life is a grindstone. Whether it grinds us down
or polishes us up depends on us.**

L. THOMAS HOLDCROFT, CANADIAN THEOLOGIAN

**Life is a train of moods like a string of beads; and
as we pass through them they prove to be many colored
lenses, which paint the world their own hue, and each
shows us only what lies in its own focus.**

RALPH WALDO EMERSON, AMERICAN WRITER

Life is just a chance to grow a soul.

A. POWELL DAVIES, BRITISH-BORN UNITARIAN MINISTER

Life is about authenticity, recognizing and honoring one's song, getting in tune with that song and singing it well.

MARGE SCHNEIDER, AUTHOR OF *A HAND IN HEALING: THE POWER OF EXPRESSIVE PUPPETRY*

The meaning of life is quite simple. Sit back, kick the cruise control into action and enjoy the trip.

TERRY "TUBESTEAK" TRACY, AMERICAN SURFER

I found out that all the important lessons in life are contained in the three rules for achieving a perfect golf swing:

Keep your head down.
Follow through.
Be born with money.

P. J. O'ROURKE, AMERICAN JOURNALIST

In three words I can sum up everything
I've learned about life: it goes on.

ROBERT FROST, AMERICAN POET

In the book of life,
the answers aren't in the back.

CHARLES SCHULZ, AMERICAN CARTOONIST

The meaning of life? It is life itself!

MAREK HALTER, POLISH NOVELIST

The Answer to the Great Question...of Life,
the Universe and Everything...(is) Forty-two.

DOUGLAS ADAMS, *THE HITCHHIKER'S GUIDE TO THE GALAXY*

Life Is...

"Life is Just a Bowl of Cherries."
LEW BROWN, RUSSIAN-BORN LYRICIST (SONG TITLE)

Life is a celebration of being here on this earth.
MARGIE KLEIN, AUTHOR'S 94-YEAR-OLD MOTHER

Life is just a collection of memories...but memories, my friends, are like starlight because memories go on forever.
C. W. MCCALL, AMERICAN STORYTELLER

Life is a roller coaster. Try to eat a light lunch.
DAVID A. SCHMALTZ, AUTHOR OF *THE BLIND MEN AND THE ELEPHANT*

 Life is the art of drawing without an eraser.
JOHN W. GARDNER, AMERICAN ADMINISTRATOR

Life is painting a picture, not creating a sum.
OLIVER WENDELL HOLMES JR., AMERICAN JURIST

Think, if you will, of your life as an art gallery and of the events in it as paintings that you have made. A week ago or a year ago or just yesterday you began a picture and today it turns up in the gallery that is your life. You stop to look at it. Is it beautiful...or is it ugly...? Whatever it is, see it as a painting in the gallery of your life, and consider that the spirit in which you paint today determines how nice your gallery looks tomorrow.

BRIAN BROWNE WALKER, *THE CRAZY DOG GUIDE OF LIFETIME HAPPINESS*

For a long time it had seemed to me that life was about to begin—real life. But there was always some obstacle in the way, something to be got through first, some unfinished business, time still to be served, a debt to be paid. Then life would begin. At last it dawned on me that these obstacles were my life.

JAMES PATTERSON, *SAM'S LETTERS TO JENNIFER*

Our life is March weather, savage and serene in one hour.

RALPH WALDO EMERSON, AMERICAN WRITER

Unrest of spirit is a mark of life; one problem after another presents itself and in the solving of them we can find our greatest pleasure.

KARL MENNINGER, AMERICAN PSYCHIATRIST

Life is to explore, to discover, to delight and be delighted.

NICOLE SCHAPIRO, AUTHOR OF *NEGOTIATING FOR YOUR LIFE*

**Life is made up of desires that seem big and vital
one minute and little and absurd the next.
I guess we get what's best for us in the end.**

ALICE CALDWELL RICE, AMERICAN WRITER

**The difference between life and the movies is that a script
has to make sense, and life doesn't.**

JOSEPH L. MANKIEWICZ, POLISH-AMERICAN SCREENWRITER

Life is absurd.

ALBERT CAMUS, FRENCH-ALGERIAN PHILOSOPHER

**Of course life is bizarre: the more bizarre it gets, the more
interesting it is. The only way to approach it is to make
yourself some popcorn and enjoy the show.**

ANONYMOUS

Life is full of infinite absurdities, which, strangely enough, do not even need to appear plausible, since they are true.

LUIGI PIRANDELLO, ITALIAN PLAYWRIGHT

Life is just one damned thing after another.

ELBERT HUBBARD, AMERICAN WRITER

Life is a crowded superhighway with bewildering cloverleaf exits on which a man is liable to find himself speeding back in the direction he came.

PETER DE VRIES, AMERICAN NOVELIST

Life is a series of steps. Things are done gradually. Every once in a while there is a giant step, but most of the time we are taking small, seemingly insignificant steps on the stairway of life.

RALPH RANSOM, *STEPS ON THE STAIRWAY*

Life is an unfoldment, and the further we travel
the more truth we can comprehend. To understand
the things that are at our door is the best preparation
for understanding those that lie beyond.

HYPATIA, EGYPTIAN MATHEMATICIAN

Life is a journey, from birth to death. If you awake to
the possibilities of your journey, it will lead you from isolation
to connection; from ignorance to knowledge; from pretense
to authenticity; and from fear to love.

SUSAN PAGE, AUTHOR OF *IF I'M SO WONDERFUL, WHY AM I STILL SINGLE?*

Life is indeed a journey. We don't have a map unless we draw
one up ourselves, and the road is filled with unknowns.
Sometimes there's smooth sailing, sometimes there are pot-
holes, detours, washouts, and never ending sections of major
construction. Sometimes we have to speed up, other times we
need to slow down, stop, wait, and even back up. But through
it all, those of us who truly know how to live are aware that,
wherever we may be, it pays to look around and enjoy the
scenery.

C. LESLIE CHARLES, AUTHOR OF *WHY IS EVERYONE SO CRANKY?*

I have found life an enjoyable, enchanting, active, and some-time terrifying experience, and I've enjoyed it completely. A lament in one ear, maybe, but always a song in the other.

SEAN O'CASEY, IRISH PLAYWRIGHT

Too often life can seem to be an unpredictable ride between birth and death: we are born without choosing, and die at any time. In between there are many entrances, exits, and detours—some bring great blessings, others great sorrow. Yet we always have some degree of choice—opportunities to fail, or to flourish. Put yourself in the driver's seat as often as possible, and stay awake behind the wheel. Life is a road trip to be experienced to the fullest!

LIAM CUNNINGHAM, AMERICAN PHOTOGRAPHER

Life itself is paradox; both meaningful and meaningless, important and insignificant, a joke and a yoke.

WES "SCOOP" NISKER, IN *CRAZY WISDOM*

Life. It's full of such sadness and sorrow, sometimes I think it's better not to be born at all! But how many people do you meet in a lifetime who were that lucky?

YIDDISH SAYING

A garden is always a series of losses
set against a few triumphs, like life itself.

MAY SARTON, BELGIAN POET

Life is tough, but I'm tougher.

ANDY ROONEY, AMERICAN NEWS COMMENTATOR

Life is easier than you'd think; all that is necessary is
to accept the impossible, do without the indispensable,
and bear the intolerable.

KATHLEEN NORRIS, AMERICAN WRITER

Life is rough for everyone.... Life isn't always fair.
Whatever it is that hits the fan, it's never evenly distributed—
some always tend to get more of it then others.

ANN LANDERS, AMERICAN ADVICE COLUMNIST

When life fits our expectations, we think of it as an
opportunity. When it does not, we think the world failed us,
not our expectations. But that is a mistake, for life will be
whatever it wants to be, and not necessarily what we want.

ARNOLD BEISSER, *FLYING WITHOUT WINGS*

Life is a sum of all your choices.

ALBERT CAMUS, FRENCH-ALGERIAN PHILOSOPHER

Life works when you choose what you got. Actually what you got is what you chose. To move on, choose.

WERNER ERHARD, FOUNDER OF EST (ERHARD SEMINARS TRAINING)

Life is an error-making and an error-correcting process, and nature in marking man's papers will grade him for wisdom as measured both by survival and by the quality of life of those who survive.

JONAS SALK, AMERICAN SCIENTIST

Life is a do over. Just because you screw up once doesn't mean you don't get a second chance.

BARRY WISHNER, AMERICAN CEO OF PROFORMANCE

The art of life is a constant readjustment to our surroundings.

KAKUZO OKAKAURA, JAPANESE PHILOSOPHER

Life is a game played on us while we are playing other games.

EVAN ESAR, AMERICAN HUMORIST

When I hear somebody sigh, "Life is hard,"
I am always tempted to ask, "Compared to what?"

SYDNEY J. HARRIS, *MAJORITY OF ONE*

Life is a jest, and all things show it;
I thought so once, now I know it.

JOHN GAY, *MY OWN EPITAPH*

Life is what happens to you while you are
busy making other plans.

JOHN LENNON, BRITISH MUSICIAN

Life is something to do when you can't get to sleep.

FRAN LEBOWITZ, *METROPOLITAN LIFE*

You only live once—but if you work it right, once is enough.

JOE E. LEWIS, AMERICAN COMEDIAN

The first forty years of life gives us the text;
the next thirty supply the commentary on it.

ARTHUR SCHOPENHAUER, GERMAN PHILOSOPHER

**Life's a tough proposition,
and the first hundred years are the hardest.**

WILSON MIZNER, AMERICAN PLAYWRIGHT

Life is the biggest bargain. We get it for nothing.

YIDDISH SAYING

That it will never come again is what makes life so sweet.

EMILY DICKINSON, AMERICAN POET

The unfortunate, yet truly exciting thing about your life, is that there is no core curriculum. The entire place is an elective.... So if there's any real advice I can give you it's this. College is something you complete. Life is something you experience.

JON STEWART, AMERICAN COMEDIAN

**Life is my college. May I graduate well,
and earn some honors!**

LOUISA MAY ALCOTT, AMERICAN WRITER

Life Isn't . . .

Life isn't about finding yourself. Life is about creating yourself.

GEORGE BERNARD SHAW, IRISH PLAYWRIGHT

Your life is not a problem to be solved but a gift to be opened.

WAYNE MULLER, AUTHOR OF *LEGACY OF THE HEART*

**Life is an enjoyable game to be played—not
a horrible problem to be solved.**

KEN KEYES, JR., AND BRUCE BURKAN, *HOW TO MAKE
YOUR LIFE WORK OR WHY AREN'T YOU HAPPY?*

**Life is not a problem to be solved once; it is a continuing
challenge to be lived day by day. Our quest is not to find
the answer but to find ways of making each
individual day a human experience.**

HAROLD S. KUSHNER, *WHEN ALL YOU'VE EVER WANTED ISN'T ENOUGH*

Life is not life unless you make mistakes.

JOAN COLLINS, BRITISH ACTOR

Life is not a problem. If we live, we live; if we die, we die; if we suffer, we suffer; it appears that we are the problem.

ALAN WATTS, BRITISH PHILOSOPHER

Life isn't a science. We make it up as we go.

AL HIRSCHFELD, AMERICAN CARICATURIST

Life is a progress, and not a station.

RALPH WALDO EMERSON, AMERICAN WRITER

Life is not dated merely by years. Events are sometimes the best calendars.

BENJAMIN DISRAELI, BRITISH STATESMAN

**Life is not long, and too much of it must not pass
in idle deliberation how it shall be spent.**

SAMUEL JOHNSON, BRITISH WRITER

**Life isn't all about what you don't have, but yet,
what you do with what you have been given.**

ROBERT M. HENSEL, SPANISH-BORN AMERICAN DISABILITY ADVOCATE

**Life is not so bad if you have plenty of luck,
a good physique and not too much imagination.**

CHRISTOPHER ISHERWOOD, BRITISH NOVELIST

Life isn't all golf.

TIGER WOODS, AMERICAN GOLFER

Life Is Like...

**Life is rather like a tin of sardines—
we're all of us looking for the key.**

ALAN BENNETT, *BEYOND THE FRINGE (STAGE REVUE)*

**Life is like a bagel. It's delicious when it's fresh and warm,
but often it's just hard. The hole in the middle is its great
mystery, and yet it wouldn't be a bagel without it.**

SEMINAR PARTICIPANT IN *A WHACK ON THE SIDE OF THE HEAD*, BY ROGER VON OECH

**Life is like a sewer. What you get out of it
depends on what you put into it.**

TOM LEHRER, AMERICAN SATIRIST

**Life is like a combination lock; your goal is to find the right
numbers, in the right order, so you can have anything you want.**

BRIAN TRACY, AMERICAN BUSINESS CONSULTANT

**Life is like an onion: You peel it off
one layer at a time, and sometimes you weep.**

CARL SANDBURG, AMERICAN POET

**My Mama always said life was like a box of chocolates.
You never know what you're gonna get.**

TOM HANKS IN *FORREST GUMP*

**Life is like riding a bicycle.
You don't fall off unless you stop pedaling.**

ANONYMOUS

**Life is like a ten-speed bike.
Most of us have gears we never use.**

CHARLES SCHULZ, CREATOR OF THE COMIC STRIP *PEANUTS*

**Life is like a dogsled team. If you ain't the lead dog,
the scenery never changes.**

LEWIS GRIZZARD, AMERICAN COMEDIAN

Life is like a library owned by an author.
In it are a few books which he wrote himself,
but most of them were written for him.

HARRY EMERSON FOSDICK, AMERICAN BAPTIST MINISTER

Life is like a mirror. You frown at it, it glares back at you;
you smile at life and it returns the smile.

RALPH RANSOM, *STEPS ON THE STAIRWAY*

Life is like a game of cards. The hand that is dealt you
represents determinism; the way you play it is free will.

JAWAHARLAL NEHRU, INDIAN PRIME MINISTER

Life is like a B-grade movie. You don't want to leave in the
middle of it, but you don't want to see it again.

TED TURNER, AMERICAN MEDIA MOGUL

Life is like music, it must be composed by ear, feeling and
instinct, not by rule.

SAMUEL BUTLER, BRITISH WRITER

Our lives are like a candle in the wind.

CARL SANDBURG, AMERICAN POET

Life is like an overlong drama through which we sit being nagged by the vague memories of having read the reviews.

JOHN UPDIKE, *THE COUP*

I think of life itself now as a wonderful play that I've written for myself...and so my purpose is to have the utmost fun playing my part.

SHIRLEY MacLAINE, AMERICAN ACTOR

Life is a moderately good play with a badly written third act.

TRUMAN CAPOTE, AMERICAN WRITER

Life's like a play: it's not the length, but the excellence of the acting that matters.

SENECA, ROMAN STATESMAN

Life is like a jigsaw puzzle but you don't have the picture on the front of the box to know what it's supposed to look like. Sometimes, you're not even sure if you have all the pieces.

Seminar participant in *A Whack on the Side of the Head*, by Roger von Oech

Life is like playing the violin solo in public and learning the instrument as one goes on.

Samuel Butler, British writer

Life is like a coin. You can spend it any way you wish, but you only spend it once.

Lillian Dickson, American missionary

Life is like a roll of toilet paper, the closer it gets to the end, the faster it goes.

Andy Rooney, American news commentator

Life Is Love

To me life has meaning because we love.

ELEANOR ROOSEVELT, AMERICAN HUMANITARIAN

**I believe that the reason of life
is for each of us simply to grow in love.**

LEO TOLSTOY, RUSSIAN NOVELIST

Where there is love there is life.

MAHATMA GANDHI, INDIAN SPIRITUAL LEADER

I have found that if you love life, life will love you back.

ARTHUR RUBINSTEIN, POLISH-AMERICAN PIANIST

**Love is the ultimate and the highest goal to which we can
aspire...salvation is through love and in love.**

VIKTOR FRANKL, AUSTRIAN PSYCHIATRIST

Life is the flower of which love is the honey.

VICTOR HUGO, FRENCH WRITER

Life in abundance comes only through great love.

ELBERT HUBBARD, AMERICAN WRITER

**If you give your life as a wholehearted response to love,
then love will wholeheartedly respond to you.**

MARIANNE WILLIAMSON, AMERICAN SPIRITUAL TEACHER

**Life is a paradise for those
who love many things with a passion.**

LEO BUSCAGLIA, ITALIAN-AMERICAN WRITER

**The absolute value of love makes life worthwhile, and so
Man's strange and difficult situation acceptable. Love cannot
save life from death; but it can fulfill life's purpose.**

ARNOLD TOYNBEE, BRITISH HISTORIAN

You will find as you look back upon your life that the moments
when you have really lived are the moments when you have
done things in the spirit of love.

HENRY DRUMMOND, SCOTTISH EVANGELICAL WRITER

There is only one happiness in life,
to love and be loved.

GEORGE SAND, FRENCH NOVELIST

Life without love is like a tree
without blossoms or fruit.

KAHLIL GIBRAN, LEBANESE POET

Keep love in your heart. A life without it is like
a sunless garden when the flowers are dead. The
consciousness of loving and being loved brings a warmth
and richness to life that nothing else can bring.

OSCAR WILDE, IRISH PLAYWRIGHT

Life is so precious. Please, please, let's love one another, live
each day, reach out to each other, be kind to each other.

JULIA ROBERTS, AMERICAN ACTOR

If you were all alone in the universe with no one to talk to, no one with which to share the beauty of the stars, to laugh with, to touch, what would be your purpose in life? It is other life, it is love, which gives your life meaning. This is harmony. We must discover the joy of each other, the joy of challenge, the joy of growth.

MITSUGI SAOTOME, JAPANESE AIKIDO MASTER

Life has taught us that love does not consist in gazing at each other but in looking outward together in the same direction.

ANTOINE DE SAINT EXUPÉRY, FRENCH WRITER

Life is short and we never have too much time for gladdening the hearts of those who are traveling the dark journey with us. Oh, be swift to love, make haste to be kind!

HENRI-FRÉDÉRIC AMIEL, SWISS WRITER

The underlying question at the end of our lives always is, "How well did I love?"

JOHN WELSHONS, AUTHOR OF *AWAKENING FROM GRIEF*

**The meaning of life is that we love one another.
The purpose of our lives, it seems to me, is to learn
how to do that, so we can create a world where
everyone's in love with everyone all the time.**

MARIANNE WILLIAMSON, AMERICAN SPIRITUAL TEACHER

**In our life there is a single color, as on an artist's palette,
which provides the meaning of life and art.
It is the color of love.**

MARC CHAGALL, RUSSIAN-BORN FRENCH PAINTER

**The supreme happiness in life is
the conviction that we are loved.**

VICTOR HUGO, FRENCH WRITER

**One word frees us of all the weight and pain of life:
That word is love.**

SOPHOCLES, GREEK PLAYWRIGHT

Love is life. And if you miss love, you miss life.

LEO BUSCAGLIA, ITALIAN-AMERICAN WRITER

Life Is a Mystery

Life is a roar of bargain and battle; but in the very heart of it there rises a mystical spiritual tone that gives meaning to the whole. It transmutes the dull details into romance.

OLIVER WENDELL HOLMES, JR., AMERICAN JURIST

Row, row, row your boat
Gently down the stream.
Merrily, merrily, merrily, merrily
Life is but a dream.

TRADITIONAL SONG

What if everything is an illusion and nothing exists?
In that case, I definitely overpaid for my carpet.

WOODY ALLEN, AMERICAN COMEDIAN

Life's meaning is a mystery.

BETTY FRIEDAN, AMERICAN FEMINIST

Life is about not knowing, having to change, taking the moment and making the best of it, without knowing what's going to happen next. Delicious ambiguity!

GILDA RADNER, AMERICAN COMEDIAN

There's nothing more ironic or strange or contradictory than life itself.

ROBERT DE NIRO, AMERICAN ACTOR

Life is an end in itself, and the only question as to whether it is worth living is whether you have enough of it.

OLIVER WENDELL HOLMES, JR., AMERICAN JURIST

The great business of life is to be, to do, to do without, and to depart.

JOHN MORLEY, BRITISH STATESMAN

Life is a great and wondrous mystery and the only thing we know that we have for sure is what is right here right now. Don't miss it.

LEO BUSCAGLIA, ITALIAN-AMERICAN WRITER

What is life? An illusion, a shadow, a story.
And the greatest good is little enough: for all life is
a dream, and dreams themselves are only dreams.

PEDRO CALDERON DE LA BARCA, SPANISH PLAYWRIGHT

The mystery of existence is the connection between our faults
and our misfortunes.

MADAME DE STAEL, FRENCH WRITER

If you want my final opinion on the mystery of life and all that,
I can give it to you in a nutshell. The universe is like a safe to
which there is a combination. But the combination is locked up
in the safe.

PETER DE VRIES, *LET ME COUNT THE WAYS*

Nobody gets to live life backward. Look ahead,
that is where your future lies.

ANN LANDERS, AMERICAN ADVICE COLUMNIST

 Life can only be understood backwards;
but it must be lived forwards.

SØREN KIERKEGAARD, DANISH PHILOSOPHER

Living is an art, not a science.
You make it up as you go along.

AL HIRSCHFELD, AMERICAN CARICATURIST

Life is the art of drawing sufficient conclusions
from insufficient premises.

SAMUEL BUTLER, BRITISH WRITER

Life is uncharted territory.
It reveals its story one moment at a time.

LEO BUSCAGLIA, ITALIAN-AMERICAN WRITER

Our life is a faint tracing on the surface of mystery.

ANNIE DILLARD, AMERICAN WRITER

Why We're Here

Why are we here? To enjoy the experience of being alive. Yes, that's it! Quite simple, really.

ED BRODOW, AUTHOR OF *BEATING THE SUCCESS TRAP*

Personally, I think the reason we are here is that it was too crowded where we were supposed to go.

STEVEN WRIGHT, AMERICAN COMEDIAN

We are here to give jobs to census takers.

MALCOLM KUSHNER, AUTHOR OF *PUBLIC SPEAKING FOR DUMMIES*

The very purpose of existence is to reconcile the glowing opinion we hold of ourselves with the appalling things that other people think about us.

QUENTIN CRISP, BRITISH WRITER AND ACTOR

"Why are we here?" That profound question can be answered in three easy words: TO WORSHIP ME.

JUDY TENUTA, AMERICAN COMEDIAN

Why are we here?

Short answer: We're here to experience the highest level of joy possible.

Long answer: We're here to fulfill our purpose. If you know what it is, you're to enjoy the journey that you've set for yourself. If your purpose is not crystal clear, then your purpose is to discover your purpose.

SUSAN SCOTT, AUTHOR OF *CREATE THE LOVE OF YOUR LIFE*

A life devoted to things is a dead life, a stump;
a God-shaped life is a flourishing tree.

PROVERBS 11:28

If you want to know why you were placed on this planet,
you must begin with God. You were born by his purpose
and for his purpose.

RICK WARREN, *THE PURPOSE DRIVEN LIFE*

To know and to serve God, of course,
is why we're here.

GARRISON KEILLOR, AMERICAN HUMORIST

**The secret of man's being is not only to live
but to have something to live for.**

FYODOR DOSTOYEVSKY, *THE BROTHERS KARAMAZOV*

**One needs something to believe in, something for which one
can have whole-hearted enthusiasm. One needs to feel that
one's life has meaning, that one is needed in this world.**

HANNAH SENESH, HUNGARIAN-JEWISH POET

**Unless you assume a God,
the question of life's purpose is meaningless.**

BERTRAND RUSSELL, BRITISH PHILOSOPHER

**To achieve a miraculous experience of life, we must embrace
a more spiritual perspective. Otherwise, we will die one day
without ever having known the real joy of living.**

MARIANNE WILLIAMSON, *THE GIFT OF CHANGE*

**Every man's life is a fairy tale
written by God's fingers.**

HANS CHRISTIAN ANDERSEN, DANISH WRITER

For everything that lives is holy,
life delights in life.

WILLIAM BLAKE, BRITISH POET

Just to be is a blessing, just to live is holy.

ABRAHAM JOSHUA HESCHEL, *THE INSECURITY OF FREEDOM*

Life becomes religious whenever we make it so: when some
new light is seen, when some deeper appreciation is felt, when
some larger outlook is gained, when some nobler purpose is
formed, when some task is well done.

SOPHIA LYON FAHS, CHINESE-BORN RELIGIOUS EDUCATOR

An authentic life is the most personal form of worship.
Everyday life has become my prayer.

SARAH BAN BREATHNACH, AMERICAN WRITER

While we are just a grain of sand in the great flow of time,
we are, each of us, unique and necessary to the
fulfillment of some cosmic plan.

KATHLEEN BREHONY, AUTHOR OF *AWAKENING AT MIDLIFE*

The goal of life is living in agreement with nature.

ZENO, GREEK PHILOSOPHER

We are here to fulfill our potential. We are born as seeds. Either we choose to nurture the seed with the right soil and the right climate, bloom into a flower and share our unique beauty with the world, or we die as a rotten seed. It is our choice.

PRAGITO DOVE, AUTHOR OF *LUNCHTIME ENLIGHTENMENT*

There is no meaning to life except the meaning man gives to his life by the unfolding of his powers.

ERICH FROMM, GERMAN-AMERICAN PSYCHOLOGIST

Life has no meaning unless one lives it with a will, at least to the limit of one's will.

PAUL GAUGUIN, FRENCH PAINTER

No pleasure philosophy, no sensuality, no place nor power, no material success can for a moment give such inner satisfaction as the sense of living for good purposes, for maintenance of integrity, for the preservation of self-approval.

MINOT SIMONS, AMERICAN MINISTER

We are here to express our unique version of life, to say, "This being, this me, is part of Life." Just the way that pine tree gives off its pine scent and says, "I'm not an oak tree or a pig. I'm a pine tree; get used to it."

NEIL FIORE, AUTHOR OF *AWAKEN YOUR STRONGEST SELF*

We can discover this meaning in life in three different ways: (1) by doing a deed; (2) by experiencing a value; and (3) by suffering.

VIKTOR FRANKL, AUSTRIAN PSYCHIATRIST

"Why are we here?" is surely the most important question human beings must face…. Our obligation is to confer meaning to life and, in doing so, overcome temptations of passivity and indifference.

ELIE WIESEL, ROMANIAN-JEWISH WRITER

The purpose of life is to live a life of purpose.

ROBERT BYRNE, AMERICAN CHESS PLAYER

The purpose of life is to listen—to yourself, to your neighbor, to your world and to God and, when the time comes, to respond in as helpful a way as you can find...from within and without.

FRED ROGERS, AMERICAN TELEVISION PERFORMER

I don't think any of us really knows why we're here. But I think we're supposed to believe we're here for a purpose.

RAY CHARLES, AMERICAN MUSICIAN

We're here to hold each other's souls...one laugh, one tear at a time...until we figure out why we are here.

SARANNE ROTHBERG, FOUNDER AND CEO, THE COMEDYCURES FOUNDATION

Why are we here? The question "why" is continually being answered by the omnipresent crows of the world— "be-CAWS, be-CAWS, be-CAWS."

WES "SCOOP" NISKER, AUTHOR OF ESSENTIAL CRAZY WISDOM

The question is not "Why are we here?" but "How should we live our lives?"

MORTIMER ADLER, AMERICAN PHILOSOFHER

Why are we here? Why aren't we more here? Why leave our life half consumed from day to day? The problem is we are not here we are only dreaming we are any where at all. And it could be such a startling brilliant dream but it ain't, just a dull interpretation of lost worlds.

STEPHEN LEVINE, AUTHOR OF *WHO DIES?*

I don't believe life has a purpose. Life is a lot of protoplasm with an urge to reproduce and continue in being.

JOSEPH CAMPBELL, *THE POWER OF MYTH*

My good friend Jacques Monod spoke often of the randomness of the cosmos. He believed everything in existence occurred by pure chance with the possible exception of his breakfast, which he felt certain was made by his housekeeper.

WOODY ALLEN, *SIDE EFFECTS*

Maybe we are part of someone's experiment to determine whether we can figure out why we are here, and our confusion, like that of rats in a maze, is the whole point.

WES "SCOOP" NISKER, AUTHOR OF *ESSENTIAL CRAZY WISDOM*

I believe our Heavenly Father invented man because
He was disappointed in the monkey.

MARK TWAIN, AMERICAN WRITER

We are here and it is now. Further than that all
human knowledge is moonshine.

H. L. MENCKEN, AMERICAN JOURNALIST

Life is nothing more than the happiness you get out of it.

JEAN ANOUILH, IN *ANTIGONE*

I believe that the very purpose of our life is to seek happiness.

DALAI LAMA, *THE ART OF HAPPINESS*

The purpose of life, after all, is to live it,
to taste experience to the utmost, to reach out eagerly
and without fear for newer and richer experiences.

ELEANOR ROOSEVELT, AMERICAN HUMANITARIAN

The purpose of life is to live it as fully as possible, and to be grateful every day for the privilege of sharing.

LEONARD BERNSTEIN, AMERICAN COMPOSER

The reason we are here is to ask "Why are we here?" and have the question go unanswered.

MARC KRAVITZ, AMERICAN ADVERTISING EXECUTIVE

There ain't no answer. There ain't going to be any answer. There never has been an answer. That's the answer.

GERTRUDE STEIN, AMERICAN WRITER

How is it possible to find meaning in a finite world, given my waist and shirt size?

WOODY ALLEN, *SIDE EFFECTS*

I was in New York's Metropolitan Museum of Art when an old woman comes up to me and says "excuse me young man. Can you tell me what time it is?" I look at my watch and say, "it's exactly two o'clock." She tells me that she had a two o'clock appointment with friends, but they aren't here. Then, she continues on, without a comma or period, that she was rarely late for appointments, knew nothing about primitive art, worked at the Bronx Botanical Gardens. I'm day-dreaming, looking at her, five-foot-two-inches, neatly dressed in a blue suit with a matching pillbox hat. In her white-gloved hand, she is carrying a handbag. Politely trying to get away, I hear her say "that's the secret of life." I know I've missed something so I ask her "what's the secret of life?" And she says "sneakers are the secret of life." I have no idea what she is talking about but as I look down more carefully I see that accompanying her Easter ensemble, she is wearing sneakers. I know I've missed something so I ask her "how are sneakers the secret of life?" And she repeats, "I wear these sneakers because they are only comfortable when you keep moving. That's the secret of life; you gotta keep moving."

CARL HAMMERSCHLAG, AUTHOR OF *THE THEFT OF THE SPIRIT*

Can you imagine what would happen if the mystery of life and our existence was solved? If all the answers, plots, characters, goals, destinies, procedures, and processes were revealed? All of a sudden God and creation would become boring.

MYLES R. BERG, *THE WONDERS OF THE WORLD AND WORD*

Who knows why we're here? No one knows. You can say you do, but you can't. All you can say is what I said. It ain't over 'til it's over. And that's all.

YOGI BERRA, AMERICAN BASEBALL PLAYER

I am here for lunch.

FRANK CHIN, CHINESE-AMERICAN WRITER

To Learn about Ourselves

**Man's main task in life is to give birth to himself,
to become what he potentially is.**

ERICH FROMM, GERMAN-AMERICAN PSYCHOLOGIST

As long as you live, keep learning how to live.

SENECA, ROMAN STATESMAN

**Never become so much of an expert that you stop gaining
expertise. View life as a continuous learning experience.**

DENIS WAITLEY, AMERICAN BUSINESS CONSJLTANT

Life is a succession of experiences sprinkled with emotions, people, places, adventures, triumphs, wonders, disappointments, puzzlements, injustices, loves, losses, and, if you pay attention, lessons that make the journey that much more savory and easily navigable along the way.

ERIKA LENKERT, AUTHOR OF THE LAST-MINUTE PARTY GIRL

Each person has his or her own purpose and distinct path, unique and separate from anyone else's. As you travel your life path, you will be presented with numerous lessons that you will need to learn in order to fulfill that purpose. The lessons you are presented with are specific to you; learning these lessons is the key to discovering and fulfilling the meaning and relevance of your own life.

CHÉRIE CARTER-SCOTT, IF LIFE IS A GAME, THESE ARE THE RULES

Life gives us not only our genetic packages, but also a certain style of character, a style of being, and our gifts uniquely equip us for certain callings, through which we both grow into our fullest humanity, and nourish the world around us.

DAVIDSON LOEHR, AMERICAN MINISTER

First of all, life is a journey…every experience is here to teach
you more fully how to be who you really are.

OPRAH WINFREY, AMERICAN TELEVISION PERFORMER

Your only obligation in any lifetime
is to be true to yourself.

RICHARD BACH, *ILLUSIONS*

The enjoyment of the journey comes by learning to love myself
despite my imperfections, limitations and vulnerabilities.

MARGE SCHNEIDER, AUTHOR OF *A HAND IN HEALING:*
THE POWER OF EXPRESSIVE PUPPETRY

The purpose of life, then, is to lovingly accept ourselves
and each other, without bias or prejudice, as we
learn to unveil the divine spark within.

BARBARA BRENNAN, AMERICAN SCIENTIST

Why are we here? To take "Life 101,"
a curriculum of life experience through which we
can awaken into the fullness of our being.

RAM DASS, AMERICAN SPIRITUAL TEACHER

If we search outside ourselves for the meaning of life, we tend never to find it. But if we center ourselves and look for meaning in life, it's always waiting for us, right here in the present moment.

BO LOZOFF, *IT'S A MEANINGFUL LIFE*

I find that when we really love and accept and approve of ourselves exactly as we are, then everything in life works.

LOUISE HAY, AMERICAN METAPHYSICAL TEACHER

Even if the patterns of my life do not conform to my preconceived vision of how I wished or expected things to be, every moment is a learning opportunity. Every moment is sacred. Every moment offers me a unique challenge. And, no matter how much I may protest, every moment is perfect for me at that time.

JEFFREY MISHLOVE, AMERICAN PARAPSYCHOLOGY RESEARCHER

There are no mistakes, no coincidences. All events are blessings given to us to learn from.

ELISABETH KÜBLER-ROSS, SWISS THANATOLOGIST

When you ask yourself, "Why am I here?" or
"Why is this happening to me?" or "What's it all about?"
turn to your spiritual primer. Ask yourself,
"What is the lesson?"

CHÉRIE CARTER-SCOTT, *IF LIFE IS A GAME, THESE ARE THE RULES*

Life is a succession of lessons
which must be lived to be understood.

RALPH WALDO EMERSON, AMERICAN WRITER

There comes a time when it lies within a man's grasp
to shape the clay of his life into the sort of thing he
wishes to be. Only the weak blame parents, the times,
lack of good fortune, or quirks of fate.

LOUIS L'AMOUR, AMERICAN WRITER

Living on this earth is such a rich experience. If we stand
back from our lives, sounds, sights and smells, experiences
profane and sublime whirl and blend deliciously into a tapestry
of lush colors and multiple textures. If we stand farther back
and look in, we can see how our life is a shining thread in a
larger tapestry, the fabric of all life.

ERIN EVERETT, EDITOR, *NEW LIFE JOURNAL*

**The meaning of our life is to experience
the divinity of ourselves and of all creatures.**

WILLIGIS JÄGER, *SEARCH FOR THE MEANING OF LIFE*

**Life is a test, a school where we come to learn and grow in our
spiritual understanding and personal development, a school
designed for each of us to reach our own unique destiny. Each of
us is here to learn, to grow, to master the challenges that we
face, and to expand our capacity for love and compassion. Taking
life on with courage, trusting that we are meant to learn from
every experience in life, is why we are here.**

JUDY TATELBAUM, AUTHOR OF *YOU DON'T HAVE TO SUFFER*

**Life is a test. It is only a test. Had this been a real life you
would have been instructed where to go and what to do.**

POSTER SAYING

**Here is a test to find whether your mission on
earth is finished; If you're alive, it isn't.**

RICHARD BACH, *ILLUSIONS*

Don't go through life, grow through life.

ERIC BUTTERWORTH, CANADIAN-BORN UNITY MINISTER

To Serve Others

**I believe we are all here to be bright torches
that light one another's way.**

BERNIE S. SIEGEL, AUTHOR OF *LOVE, MEDICINE AND MIRACLES*

**Each of us has a spark of life inside us, and our highest
endeavor ought to be to set off that spark in one another.**

KENNY AUSUBEL, AMERICAN SOCIAL ENTREPRENEUR

**We're not primarily put on this earth to see through one another,
but to see one another through.**

PETER DE VRIES, AMERICAN NOVELIST

Only a life lived for others is a life worthwhile.

ALBERT EINSTEIN, GERMAN-BORN PHYSICIST

**My only real answer to "What's life?" is:
"If you know my life you will know my answer.
And if I know your life, I'll know yours."**

DAVID KUNDTZ, AUTHOR OF *STOPPING: HOW TO
BE STILL WHEN YOU HAVE TO KEEP GOING*

Life is an exuberant gift from a Divine power that can't resist sharing the miraculous experience of existence with others.

JESSICA PRENTICE, AMERICAN CHEF

Most of all, it's about using your life to touch or poison other people's hearts in such a way that could have never occurred alone. Only you choose the way those hearts are affected, and those choices are what life's all about.

ANONYMOUS

Life is partly what we make it, and partly what it is made by the friends whom we choose.

TEHYI HSIEH, AUTHOR OF *CONFUCIUS SAID IT FIRST*

For me, life is speaking for those who no longer can.

NICOLE SCHAPIRO, AUTHOR OF *NEGOTIATING FOR YOUR LIFE*

What's life?

The short answer: a cereal.

The long answer: an opportunity for us all to grow physically, spiritually and emotionally within ourselves and through the interactions with others.

RON CULBERSON, AUTHOR OF *IS YOUR GLASS LAUGH FULL?*

The journey is not about helping ourselves, but about helping others. We do best when we use our own skills to make a positive difference in the lives of others. When we do this, we bring enjoyment, hope and fulfillment to others, but we also find that we enjoy the journey more than we ever could have imagined.

DAVE LIEBER, FORT WORTH (TX) *STAR-TELEGRAM* COLUMNIST

The more you focus on making others happy, the less self-focused you'll become and the more cheerful you'll be.

SOL GORDON AND HAROLD BRECHER, *LIFE IS UNCERTAIN...EAT DESSERT FIRST!*

What's a life, anyway? We're born, we live a little while, we die. A spider's life can't help being something of a mess, with all this trapping and eating flies. By helping you, perhaps I was trying to lift up my life a trifle. Heaven knows anyone's life can stand a little of that.

E. B. WHITE, *CHARLOTTE'S WEB*

If you have made another person on this earth smile, your life has been worthwhile.

MARY CHRISTELLE MACALUSO, *GOD KNOWS BEST ABOUT JOY*

To enjoy the journey is to leap into people's lives.
To enjoy the journey is to give until the stretch is a sacrifice....
The question always is; what is it in life that will pull
you out of your seat to be brave, risk and serve?

JANIE JASIN, AUTHOR OF *THE LITTLEST CHRISTMAS TREE*

We make a living by what we get,
but we make a life by what we give.

WINSTON CHURCHILL, BRITISH STATESMAN

When it's all over, it's not who you were.
It's whether you made a difference.

BOB DOLE, AMERICAN POLITICIAN

It's loving and giving that make life worth living.

POPULAR SAYING

If I can stop one heart from breaking,
I shall not live in vain.
If I can ease one life the aching,
Or cool one pain,
Or help one fainting robin
Unto his nest again,
I shall not live in vain.

EMILY DICKINSON, AMERICAN POET

Each of us was placed here for a special purpose. I believe that it is each person's responsibility to determine what he or she can do to make the world a better place—and then go out and do it.

ROSS PEROT, AMERICAN BUSINESSMAN

Whatever the reasons for our being here, surely one of them must be to give us the opportunity to do something, at least in some small way, to make the world a better place.

CLEVELAND AMORY, AMERICAN WRITER

Service is what life is all about.

MARIAN WRIGHT EDELMAN, AMERICAN LAWYER

**When people are serving,
life is no longer meaningless.**

JOHN W. GARDNER, AMERICAN ADMINISTRATOR

A man who becomes conscious of the responsibility he bears toward a human being who affectionately waits for him, or to an unfinished work, will never be able to throw away his life. He knows the "why" for his existence, and will be able to bear almost any "how."

VIKTOR FRANKL, AUSTRIAN PSYCHIATRIST

I think the purpose of life is to be useful, to be responsible, to be honorable, to be compassionate. It is, after all, to matter: to count, to stand for something, to have made some difference that you lived at all.

LEO ROSTEN, AMERICAN HUMORIST

**I've learned that people will forget what you said,
people will forget what you did, but people will
never forget how you made them feel.**

MAYA ANGELOU, AMERICAN POET

The life I touch for good or ill will touch another life, and that in turn another, until who knows where the trembling stops or in what far place my touch will be felt.

FREDERICK BUECHNER, AMERICAN WRITER

I am of the opinion that my life belongs to the community, and as long as I live it is my privilege to do for it whatever I can.

GEORGE BERNARD SHAW, IRISH PLAYWRIGHT

We don't accomplish anything in this world alone...and whatever happens is the result of the whole tapestry of one's life and all the weavings of individual threads from one to another that creates something.

SANDRA DAY O'CONNOR, AMERICAN JUDGE

We are here on earth to do good for others.
What the others are here for, I don't know.

W. H. AUDEN, BRITISH POET

The purpose of life...is to be useful, to be honorable, to be compassionate, to have it make some difference that you have lived and lived well.

RALPH WALDO EMERSON, AMERICAN WRITER

One's life has value so long as one attributes value to the life
of others by means of love, friendship (and) compassion.

SIMONE DE BEAUVOIR, FRENCH WRITER

Life's meaning amounts to how
we actually manage to live it with others.

ROBERT COLES, AMERICAN PSYCHIATRIST

We are here to add what we can to,
not to get what we can from, life.

WILLIAM OSLER, CANADIAN PHYSICIAN

The influence of each human being on others in this life
is a kind of immortality.

JOHN QUINCY ADAMS, U.S. PRESIDENT

To Live Fully

Life itself is the proper binge.

JULIA CHILD, AMERICAN CHEF

Life loves the liver of it.

MAYA ANGELOU, AMERICAN WRITER

Live life to the fullest.

ERNEST HEMINGWAY, AMERICAN WRITER

**A man who dares to waste one hour of life
has not discovered the value of life.**

CHARLES DARWIN, BRITISH NATURALIST

May you live all the days of your life.

JONATHAN SWIFT, ANGLO-IRISH SATIRIST

Life is too deep for words, so don't try to describe it, just live it.

C. S. LEWIS, BRITISH WRITER

We are misled from early childhood to think that life is something you get through. Life is something to be in.

DUSTIN HOFFMAN, AMERICAN ACTOR

Life leaps like a geyser for those willing to drill through the rock of inertia.

ALEXIS CARREL, FRENCH SURGEON

Life is a festival only to the wise.

RALPH WALDO EMERSON, AMERICAN WRITER

To say yes, you have to sweat and roll up your sleeves and plunge both hands into life up to the elbows.

JEAN ANOUILH, FRENCH PLAYWRIGHT

Life is a dance. Squeeze the juice out of each moment and we find our authentic self. There is no greater benediction.

PRAGITO DOVE, AUTHOR OF *LUNCHTIME ENLIGHTENMENT*

"What came over you to make you dance like that?"
"What could I do, boss? My joy was choking me. I had to find
some outlet. And what sort of outlet? Words? Pff!"

NIKOS KAZANTZAKIS, *ZORBA THE GREEK*

Life is about dancing together or
dancing apart but just keep dancing.

NICOLE SCHAPIRO, AUTHOR OF *NEGOTIATING FOR YOUR LIFE*

Dancing is no mere translation or abstraction from life;
it is life itself.

HAVELOCK ELLIS, BRITISH PSYCHOLOGIST

And we should consider every day lost
on which we have not danced at least once.

FRIEDRICH NIETZSCHE, GERMAN PHILOSOPHER

On with the dance, let joy be unconfined,
is my motto; whether there's any dance to dance
or any joy to unconfine.

MARK TWAIN, AMERICAN WRITER

Try as much as possible to be wholly alive,
with all your might, and when you laugh, laugh like hell
and when you get angry, get good and angry.
Try to be alive. You will be dead soon enough.

WILLIAM SAROYAN, AMERICAN WRITER

Too many people are thinking of security instead of
opportunity. They seem to be more afraid of life than death.

JAMES F. BYMES, AMERICAN POLITICIAN

The tragedy of life is not so much what men suffer,
but rather what they miss.

THOMAS CARLYLE, SCOTTISH ESSAYIST

Look, I really don't want to wax philosophic, but I will say that
if you're alive, you got to flap your arms and legs, you got to
jump around a lot, you got to make a lot of noise because life is
the very opposite of death. And therefore, as I see it, if you're
quiet, you're not living. You've got to be noisy, or at least your
thoughts should be noisy and colorful and lively.

MEL BROOKS, AMERICAN ACTOR

**Life is a great big canvas, and you
should throw all the paint on it you can.**

DANNY KAYE, AMERICAN ACTOR

**Life should be lived so vividly and so intensely that thoughts
of another life, or of a longer life, are not necessary.**

MARJORY STONEMAN DOUGLAS, AMERICAN WRITER

**The person who has lived the most is not the one
with the most years, but the one with the richest experiences.**

JEAN-JACQUES ROUSSEAU, SWISS-BORN FRENCH PHILOSOPHER

**We live in deeds, not years; in thoughts, not breaths;
In feelings, not in figures on a dial.
We should count time by heart-throbs. He most lives
Who thinks most, feels the noblest, acts the best.**

PHILIP JAMES BAILEY, BRITISH POET

**Life is not measured by the number of breaths we take,
but by the moments that take our breath away.**

ANONYMOUS

Step outside of your comfort zone often, express your truth with others, proactively love and be loved, explore, rejoice in everyday wonders, don't take things personally; fully feel, express, and release pain and anger; seek and express joy; don't let fear stop you from pursuing your dreams; be "game" for life, dismiss unnecessary drama, make a point of doing what you love, pamper yourself and others, play and laugh often, decide that true richness is a fulfilling life rather than a bank account figure, find and learn from life's "lessons," roll with the punches, and when all else fails, when angry: beat the s**t out of pillows until your arms go limp with fatigue and when sad, turn up your favorite song full blast and dance like crazy. It does the trick every time.

ERIKA LENKERT, AUTHOR OF *THE LAST-MINUTE PARTY GIRL*

I would urge you to be as imprudent as you dare.
BE BOLD, BE BOLD, BE BOLD.

SUSAN SONTAG, AMERICAN WRITER

Find something that moves you or pisses you off, and do something about it. Put your self out there. Be brave. Be bold. Take action. You have a voice. Speak up, especially when something tries to keep you silent. Take a stand for what's right. Raise a ruckus and make a change. You may not always be popular, but you'll be part of something larger and bigger and greater than yourself. Besides, making history is extremely cool.

SAMUEL L. JACKSON, AMERICAN ACTOR

Only when we are no longer afraid
do we begin to live.

DOROTHY THOMPSON, AMERICAN JOURNALIST

Do not be too timid and squeamish about your actions.
All life is an experiment.

RALPH WALDO EMERSON, AMERICAN WRITER

Life is a promise; fulfill it.

MOTHER TERESA, ALBANIAN CATHOLIC NUN

I could not, at any age, be content to take my place by
the fireside and simply look on. Life was meant to be lived.
Curiosity must be kept alive. One must never,
for whatever reason, turn his back on life.

ELEANOR ROOSEVELT, AMERICAN HUMANITARIAN

Life is best experienced with a sense of awe, wonder
and discovery. Go about life with a child's curiosity.
The universe is more spectacular than you can imagine.

TOM GREGORY, *THE MEANING OF LIFE*

People say that what we're all seeking is a meaning for life....
I think what we're seeking is an experience of being alive,
so that our life experiences on the purely physical plane will
have resonances within our innermost being and reality,
so that we can actually feel the rapture of being alive.

JOSEPH CAMPBELL, *THE POWER OF MYTH*

Late on the third day, at the very moment when, at sunset,
we were making our way through a herd of hippopotamuses,
there flashed upon my mind, unforeseen and unsought,
the phrase, "Reverence for Life."

ALBERT SCHWEITZER, GERMAN THEOLOGIAN

Develop an interest in life as you see it; the people,
things, literature, music—the world is so rich,
simply throbbing with rich treasures, beautiful souls
and interesting people. Forget yourself.

HENRY MILLER, AMERICAN WRITER

The longer I live, the more beautiful life becomes.

FRANK LLOYD WRIGHT, AMERICAN ARCHITECT

Life begets life. Energy creates energy. It is
by spending oneself that one becomes rich.

SARAH BERNHARDT, FRENCH ACTOR

Is not life a hundred times
too short for us to bore ourselves?

FRIEDRICH NIETZSCHE, GERMAN PHILOSOPHER

There was never yet an uninteresting life.
Such a thing is an impossibility. Inside of the dullest
exterior there is a drama, a comedy and a tragedy.

MARK TWAIN, AMERICAN WRITER

To live is so startling it leaves little time for anything else.

EMILY DICKINSON, AMERICAN POET

There are only two ways to live your life.
One is as though nothing is a miracle.
The other is as though everything is a miracle.

ALBERT EINSTEIN, GERMAN-BORN PHYSICIST

What we call the secret of happiness is no more a secret
than our willingness to choose life.

LEO BUSCAGLIA, ITALIAN-AMERICAN WRITER

When making your choice in life, do not neglect to live.

SAMUEL JOHNSON, BRITISH WRITER

Man is born to live, not to prepare for life.

BORIS PASTERNAK, *DOCTOR ZHIVAGO*

People do not live nowadays—they get
about ten percent out of life.

ISADORA DUNCAN, AMERICAN DANCER

Live all you can; it's a mistake not to. It doesn't much matter
what you do in particular, so long as you have had your life.
If you haven't had that, what have you had?

HENRY JAMES, AMERICAN WRITER

Dost thou love life? Then do not squander time,
for that's the stuff life is made of.

BENJAMIN FRANKLIN, AMERICAN STATESMAN

Life is ours to be spent, not to be saved.

D. H. LAWRENCE, BRITISH WRITER

I decided long ago never to look at the right hand of the menu
or the price tag of clothes—otherwise I would starve, naked.

HELEN HAYES, AMERICAN ACTOR

What good are vitamins? Eat four lobsters,
eat a pound of caviar—live!

ARTHUR RUBINSTEIN, POLISH-AMERICAN PIANIST

Life is short. Eat dessert first.

POPULAR SAYING

**Life is too short to do anything for oneself
that one can pay others to do for one.**

W. SOMERSET MAUGHAM, BRITISH WRITER

Life is too short to stuff a mushroom.

SHIRLEY CONRAN, BRITISH JOURNALIST

If we really want to live we must have the courage to recognize that life is ultimately very short and that everything we do counts. When it is the evening of our life we will hopefully have a chance to look back and say: "It was worthwhile because I have really lived."

ELISABETH KÜBLER-ROSS, SWISS THANATOLOGIST

**To enjoy life more fully you must keep reminding yourself
that life is too short to waste on unhappiness.**

SOL GORDON AND HAROLD BRECHER, *LIFE IS UNCERTAIN...EAT DESSERT FIRST!*

I like living. I have sometimes been wildly, despairingly, acutely miserable, racked with sorrow, but through it all I still know quite certainly that just to be alive is a grand thing.

AGATHA CHRISTIE, BRITISH WRITER

Live as if you were to die tomorrow....
Learn as if you were to live forever.

MAHATMA GANDHI, INDIAN SPIRITUAL LEADER

If my doctor told me I had only six minutes to live,
I wouldn't brood. I'd type a little faster.

ISAAC ASIMOV, RUSSIAN-BORN AMERICAN WRITER

Remember, life is not what happens to you but what you make of what happens to you. Everyone dies, but not everyone fully lives. Too many people are having "near-life experiences."

ANONYMOUS

People's whole lives do pass in front of their eyes
before they die. The process is called 'living'.

TERRY PRATCHETT, BRITISH WRITER

Life is either a daring adventure or nothing.

HELEN KELLER, AMERICAN WRITER

It matters not how long we live, but how.

PHILIP JAMES BAILEY, BRITISH POET

It is good to have an end to journey toward;
but it is the journey that matters, in the end.

URSULA K. LE GUIN, AMERICAN WRITER

Live your life and forget your age.

NORMAN VINCENT PEALE, AMERICAN RELIGIOUS LEADER

Our care should not be to have lived long
as to have lived enough.

SENECA, ROMAN STATESMAN

It is better to wear out than to rust out.

GEORGE WHITEFIELD, BRITISH MINISTER

There is no cure for birth or death, save to enjoy the interval.

GEORGE SANTAYANA, AMERICAN PHILOSOPHER

We are not born to survive. Only to live.

W. S. MERWIN, AMERICAN WRITER

And in the end, it's not the years in your life that count. It's the life in your years.

ABRAHAM LINCOLN, U.S. PRESIDENT

You can't do anything about the length of your life, but you can do something about its width and depth.

H. L. MENCKEN, AMERICAN JOURNALIST

I don't want to get to the end of my life and find that I lived just the length of it. I want to have lived the width of it as well.

DIANE ACKERMAN, AMERICAN POET

**Let us so live that when we come to die
even the undertaker will be sorry.**

MARK TWAIN, *PUDD'NHEAD WILSON*

**When you were born, you cried and the world
rejoiced; live your life so that when you die,
the world cries and you rejoice.**

CHEROKEE SAYING

How to Enjoy the Journey

Life is to be enjoyed, not just endured.

GORDON B. HINCKLEY, AMERICAN RELIGIOUS LEADER

**The greatest act of revolution in contemporary life,
is to come to every day with joy.**

CARL HAMMERSCHLAG, AUTHOR OF *HEALING CEREMONIES*

**When you think you've had all the joy you can tolerate, you've
only reached your limit, not joy's. Use that moment to expand
your limit. Don't just increase joy by a little. Double it. Then,
double that. Discover that your capacity to know joy is as
limitless as joy itself.**

JOHN-ROGER AND PETER MCWILLIAMS, IN *LIFE 101*

**Write it on your heart that every day
is the best day in the year.**

RALPH WALDO EMERSON, AMERICAN WRITER

**This is the day the Lord has made.
We will rejoice and be glad in it.**

PSALMS 118:24

One of the greatest gifts God has given you is the ability to enjoy pleasure.... He wants you to enjoy life, not just endure it.

RICK WARREN, *THE PURPOSE DRIVEN LIFE*

There is too much emphasis on success and failure, and too little on how a person grows as he works. Enjoy the journey, enjoy every moment, and quit worrying about winning and losing.

MATT BIONDI, AMERICAN OLYMPIC SWIMMER

All of the animals except for man know that the principle business of life is to enjoy it.

SAMUEL BUTLER, BRITISH WRITER

If man could only realize that God created men and animals to enjoy life, not to destroy it, then man most probably would be a lot happier.

ISAAC BASHEVIS SINGER, POLISH-BORN WRITER

Think of your life as if it were a banquet where you would behave graciously. When dishes are passed to you, extend your hand and yourself to a moderate portion. If a dish should pass you by, enjoy what is already on your plate. Or if the dish hasn't been passed to you yet, patiently wait your turn.

EPICTETUS, *MANUAL FOR LIVING*

My advice to you is not to inquire why or whither, but just enjoy your ice cream while it's on your plate—that's my philosophy.

THORNTON WILDER, *THE SKIN OF OUR TEETH*

There are two things to aim at in life:
first to get what you want; and, after that, to enjoy it.
Only the wisest of mankind achieve the second.

LOGAN PEARSALL SMITH, *AFTERTHOUGHTS*

I finally figured out the only reason
to be alive is to enjoy it.

RITA MAE BROWN, AMERICAN WRITER

No man is a failure who is enjoying life.

WILLIAM FEATHER, AMERICAN WRITER

Enjoy life...the alternative is just so unpleasant.... And stop spending so damn much time analyzing, whining, kvetching.

SUSAN ROANE, AUTHOR OF *HOW TO CREATE YOUR OWN LUCK*

"Sing More, Complain Less"

MATT WEINSTEIN AND LUKE BARBER, CHAPTER TITLE IN *WORK LIKE YOUR DOG*

Don't slow down for yellow lights, buy cereal with a prize in the box and always control the remote.

MALCOLM KUSHNER, AUTHOR OF *PUBLIC SPEAKING FOR DUMMIES*

How can we enjoy the journey?
Short answer: Sex, drugs and rock & roll.
Long answer: By using our gifts and skills in a way that enhances our own life and adds value to the lives of others.

RON CULBERSON, AUTHOR OF *IS YOUR GLASS LAUGH FULL?*

Find your bliss, pursue what gives you the most joy in life, support others to do the same, and make absolutely certain that your life is not harming any other person or diminishing the freedom of others to find and pursue their bliss!

SUSAN PAGE, AUTHOR OF *WHY TALKING IS NOT ENOUGH*

Have interesting failures…. If you need to have a personal crisis have it now. Don't wait until midlife, when it will take longer to resolve…. Don't pity yourselves. Lighten up. Seek people with a sense of humor. Avoid humorless people—and do not marry one, for God's sake.

GARRISON KEILLOR, AMERICAN HUMORIST

The most wasted of all days is that
during which one has not laughed.

NICOLAS DE CHAMFORT, FRENCH WRITER

Life is duck soup…and we are the laughingstock.

SWAMI BEYONDANANDA, *DUCK SOUP FOR THE SOUL*

Life is a tragedy when seen in close-up,
but a comedy in long-shot.

CHARLIE CHAPLIN, BRITISH ACTOR

I have always felt that laughter in the face of reality is
probably the finest sound there is and will last until the day
when the game is called on account of darkness. In this world,
a good time to laugh is any time you can.

LINDA ELLERBEE, AMERICAN JOURNALIST

**We are all here for a spell;
get all the good laughs you can.**

WILL ROGERS, AMERICAN HUMORIST

**Always laugh when you can.
It is cheap medicine.**

LORD BYRON, BRITISH POET

**That man is a success who has lived well,
laughed often and loved much.**

ROBERT LOUIS STEVENSON, SCOTTISH NOVELIST

True life lies in laughter, love and work.

ELBERT HUBBARD, AMERICAN WRITER

Take time to laugh, cry and be silent.

PRAGITO DOVE, AUTHOR OF *LUNCHTIME ENLIGHTENMENT*

Laugh it off, laugh it off; it's all part of life's rich pageant.

ARTHUR MARSHALL, *THE GAMES MISTRESS*

I call no man wise until he has made the progress from the wisdom of knowledge to the wisdom of foolishness, and become a laughing philosopher, feeling first life's tragedy and then life's comedy.

LIN YUTANG, *THE IMPORTANCE OF LIVING*

Life is a mannafestival, the FUNdamentalist scriptures tell us, and it is our mannafest destiny to manifest manna— and to have fun doing it.

SWAMI BEYONDANANDA, *DUCK SOUP FOR THE SOUL*

The comic spirit masquerades in all things we say and do. We are each a clown and do not need to put on a white face.

JAMES HILLMAN, *THE DREAM AND THE UNDERWORLD*

The secret of life is play. Play and humor are what refines and enhances our joy.

SUSAN SCOTT, AUTHOR OF *CREATE THE LOVE OF YOUR LIFE*

Without an active spirit of play your rocket never gets off the ground. It fizzles and sputters around in the driveway.

CY EBERHART, AMERICAN CLERGYMAN

Every good journey needs a GPS system. Not a global positioning satellite but a Gotta Play Some system. Whatever pressures, demands, expectations and heartache we have in our lives, we need to take time out to play.

SCOTT FRIEDMAN, AUTHOR OF *PUNCHLINES, PITFALLS AND POWERFUL PROGRAMS*

Do not take life too seriously. You will never get out of it alive.

ELBERT HUBBARD, AMERICAN WRITER

Life is too short for men to take it seriously.

GEORGE BERNARD SHAW, *BACK TO METHUSELAH*

The one serious conviction that a man should have is that nothing should be taken too seriously.

NICHOLAS MURRAY BUTLER, AMERICAN EDUCATOR

Not a shred exists in favor of the idea that life is serious.

BRENDAN GILL, AMERICAN WRITER

Don't worry, be happy.

MEYER BABA, INDIAN SPIRITUAL TEACHER

He who would travel happily must travel light.

ANTOINE DE SAINT-EXUPÉRY, FRENCH WRITER

Loosen Up:
It's not so important to be serious as it is to be
serious about the important things. The monkey wears
an expression of seriousness that would do credit to any
great scholar. But the monkey is serious because
he itches. What can you take less seriously?

ROGER VON OECH, *CREATIVE WHACK PACK* (CARD GAME)

The highest form of bliss is living with a certain degree of folly.

ERASMUS, DUTCH HUMANIST

As soon as you have made a thought, laugh at it.

LAO-TZU, CHINESE PHILOSOPHER

How we can enjoy the journey?
By connecting with others no matter how brief the encounter.
When two spirits join in the moment, there is no pain, fear,
or anger—only joy, hope, and love!

JACKI KWAN, AUTHOR OF *ALMOST HOME: EMBRACING THE
MAGICAL CONNECTION BETWEEN POSITIVE HUMOR & SPIRITUALITY*

We enjoy the journey by emphasizing those qualities
in our lives which acknowledge, or demonstrate, our essential
Oneness with ALL forms.... We are most happy when we feel
most connected.... Conversely, we are most unhappy
when we feel disconnected, isolated and alone.

JOHN WELSHONS, AUTHOR OF *AWAKENING FROM GRIEF*

How can we enjoy the journey? By WO-HE-LO.
This is a short way to say Work, Health and Love.
This is the motto of the Camp Fire Girls.

ELIZABETH PROVIDENTY, AUTHOR'S 95-YEAR-OLD MOTHER-IN-LAW

Happiness doesn't require much, just an easy attitude 'bout
yourself and life, a few interests, some people who love you
and doing things that make you feel good.

BOBBY MCFERRIN, *DON'T WORRY, BE HAPPY*

You never find happiness until you stop looking for it.

CHUANG TZU, CHINESE PHILOSOPHER

Belong...to yourself, to the earth, to others.
Above all, engage in "radical self-acceptance."

SANDRA SCHRIFT, AMERICAN SPEECH CAREER COACH

The first and great commandment is: Don't let them scare you.

ELMER DAVIS, *BUT WE WERE BORN FREE*

Life has two rules: number 1, Never quit!; number 2,
Always remember rule number 1.

DUKE ELLINGTON, AMERICAN MUSICIAN

Living is a form of not being sure, not knowing what next
or how.... The artist never entirely knows. We guess. We may
be wrong, but we take leap after leap in the dark.

AGNES DE MILLE, AMERICAN CHOREOGRAPHER

Don't be afraid to take a big step if one is indicated.
You can't cross a chasm in two small jumps.

DAVID LLOYD GEORGE, BRITISH STATESMAN

Nothing in life is to be feared.
It is only to be understood.

MARIE CURIE, POLISH-BORN FRENCH CHEMIST

How we can enjoy the journey?
Accomplish, create, celebrate, and do the things you
really want to do. Then after you have done it all,
then tell your critics to go to Hell because they are
only jealous that you did it all and they didn't.

RICK SEGEL, AUTHOR OF *RETAIL BUSINESS KIT FOR DUMMIES*

The greatest pleasure in life
is to do what people say you cannot do.

WALTER BAGEHOT, BRITISH ECONOMIST

Run from anyone who tells you he knows the truth, anyone
who touts a party line, anyone who says he has the answer.

CRAIG WILSON, *USA TODAY* COLUMNIST

Accept no one's definition of your life,
but define yourself.

HARVEY FIERSTEIN, AMERICAN ACTOR

In the first third, until about 25, have fun.
In the second third, from about 25-50, get married,
have kids. In the third third, from about 50-75, trim your
sails to match your finances. In the fourth third, from 75+,
you're on your own. Just don't kick dust in our eyes!

GORDON BURGETT, AUTHOR OF *HOW TO PLAN A GREAT SECOND LIFE*

If you get gloomy, just take an hour off and sit and
think how much better this world is than hell. Of course,
it won't cheer you up if you expect to go there.

DON MARQUIS, AMERICAN HUMORIST

The highest of wisdom is continual cheerfulness: such a state,
like the region above the moon, is always clear and serene.

MICHEL DE MONTAIGNE, FRENCH ESSAYIST

He that is of a merry heart hath a continual feast.

PROVERBS 15:15

Cheer up. Life isn't everything.

MIKE NICHOLS, GERMAN-BORN AMERICAN DIRECTOR

Alter Your Attitude

Alter your life by altering your attitudes.

WILLIAM JAMES, AMERICAN PSYCHOLOGIST

What is life but what a man is thinking all day?

RALPH WALDO EMERSON, AMERICAN WRITER

**The moment we awaken in the morning we can determine
the mood of the day, just as a sailor sets his sails and,
regardless of the wind direction, establishes
the course which his ship will take.**

LIONEL A. WHISTON, *ENJOY THE JOURNEY*

**Some folks go through life pleased that the glass is half full.
Others spend a lifetime lamenting that it's half-empty.
The truth is, there is a glass with a certain volume
of liquid in it. From there, it's up to you!**

JAMES S. VUOCOLO, AMERICAN SELF-IMPROVEMENT COACH

**It's not the load that breaks you down,
it's the way you carry it.**

LENA HORNE, AMERICAN SINGER

**Things themselves don't hurt or hinder us. Nor do other
people. How we view these things is another matter. It is
our attitudes and reactions that give us trouble.**

EPICTETUS, *MANUAL FOR LIVING*

**The art of life isn't controlling what happens,
which is impossible; it's using what happens.**

GLORIA STEINEM, IN *MOVING BEYOND WORDS*

**The principle of life is that life responds by corresponding;
your life becomes the thing you have decided it shall be.**

RAYMOND CHARLES BARKER, AMERICAN MINISTER

**It's a funny thing about life; if you refuse to accept
anything but the best, you very often get it.**

W. SOMERSET MAUGHAM, BRITISH WRITER

Most of the shadows of this life are caused by
standing in one's own sunshine.

RALPH WALDO EMERSON, AMERICAN WRITER

Be not afraid of life. Believe that life is worth living,
and your belief will help create that fact.

WILLIAM JAMES, AMERICAN PHILOSOPHER

That life is worth living is the most necessary of assumptions,
and were it not assumed, the most impossible of conclusions.

GEORGE SANTAYANA, SPANISH PHILOSOPHER

How we spend our days is, of course,
how we spend our lives.

ANNIE DILLARD, AMERICAN WRITER

Whatever is at the center of our life will be the source of our
security, guidance, wisdom, and power.

STEPHEN COVEY, AMERICAN WRITER

What we are today comes from our thoughts of yesterday,
and our present thoughts build our life of tomorrow:
Our life is the creation of our mind.

BUDDHA

Our life is what our thoughts make it.

MARCUS AURELIUS, ROMAN EMPEROR

A great way to enjoy the journey more is to mindfully focus
on the positive side of everything every step of the way.

SUSAN SCOTT, AUTHOR OF *CREATE THE LOVE OF YOUR LIFE*

We all have unwanted thoughts pop into our head from time to
time. But we also have the ongoing opportunity to choose the
thoughts we give precedence to. And the more attention we give
this process, the more control we have over creating our dream
life. We know that good thoughts create a good life. Ain't it great!

RANDY GAGE, AUTHOR OF *PROSPERITY MIND*

If one thinks that one is happy,
that is enough to be happy.

MADAME DE LA FAYETTE, FRENCH WRITER

**The secret of life is not to do what you like
but to like what you do.**

ANONYMOUS

**Learn to wish that everything
should come to pass exactly as it does.**

EPICTETUS, GREEK PHILOSOPHER

**The art of living is always
to make a good thing out of a bad thing.**

E. F. SCHUMACHER, *A GUIDE TO THE PERPLEXED*

**Life is 10 percent what happens to me and
90 percent how I react to it.**

LOU HOLTZ, AMERICAN FOOTBALL COACH

**It is not the events in our lives that do us in,
but the choices we make about how we come to them,
that brings us joy on the journey.**

CARL HAMMERSCHLAG, AUTHOR OF *THE DANCING HEALERS*

The important thing in life is not to have a good hand
but to play it well.

LOUIS N. FORTIN, FRENCH WRITER

We will often find compensation if we think more of what life
has given us and less about what life has taken away.

WILLIAM BARCLAY, SCOTTISH THEOLOGIAN

The art of living is the highest calling of all.
If we start seeing our life as a work of art-in-progress,
we will find that our attitude toward our life will change.

ALEXANDRA STODDARD, *MAKING CHOICES*

There are two ways to approach life—
as victim or as gallant fighter.

MERLE SHAIN, IN *365 REFLECTIONS ON BEING SINGLE*

The art of life is to know how to enjoy
a little and to endure much.

WILLIAM HAZLITT, BRITISH WRITER

It's better to light a candle than to curse the darkness.

CHINESE PROVERB

However mean your life is, meet it and live; do not shun it and call it hard names. It is not so bad as you are. It looks poorest when you are richest. The faultfinder will find faults even in Paradise. Love your life, poor as it is. You may perchance have pleasant, thrilling, glorious hours, even in a poorhouse.

HENRY DAVID THOREAU, AMERICAN WRITER

It is not that there is no evil, accidents, deformity, pettiness, hatred. It's that there is a broader view. Evil exists in the part. Perfection exists in the whole. Discord is seeing near-sightedly. And I can choose this broader view—not that I always should— but I always can.

HUGH PRATHER, *NOTES TO MYSELF*

Life doesn't require that we be the best—only that we try our best.

H. JACKSON BROWN, JR., AUTHOR OF *LIFE'S LITTLE INSTRUCTION BOOK*

"I have done my best." That is about all the philosophy of living one needs.

LIN YUTANG, CHINESE WRITER

Be in the Moment

Life can be found only in the present moment. The past is gone, the future is not yet here, and if we do not go back to ourselves in the present moment, we cannot be in touch with life.

THICH NHAT HANH, VIETNAMESE BUDDHIST MONK

Life is made up of years that mean nothing and the moments that mean it all.

C. P. SNOW, BRITISH SCIENTIST

Life is a series of seconds; a series of events; a series of opportunities; and a series of life-giving moments. As we live fully each moment we breath a fullness not only into our own life but into the lives of all we touch and into the very universe itself.

ANNE BRYAN SMOLLIN, AUTHOR OF *TICKLE YOUR SOUL*

Life isn't a matter of milestones, but of moments.

ROSE FITZGERALD KENNEDY, AMERICAN PHILANTHROPIST

The happiness of life is made up of minute fractions—the little, soon-forgotten charities of a kiss or smile, a kind look or heartfelt compliment.

SAMUEL TAYLOR COLERIDGE, BRITISH POET

This—this was what made life: a moment of quiet, the water falling in the fountain, the girl's voice...a moment of captured beauty. He who is truly wise will never permit such moments to escape.

LOUIS L'AMOUR, AMERICAN WRITER

Live today, forget the past.

GREEK PROVERB

Look at life through the windshield, not the rear-view mirror.

BYRD BAGGETT, AMERICAN LEADERSHIP COACH

The art of living...is neither careless drifting on the one hand nor fearful clinging to the past on the other. It consists in being sensitive to each moment, in regarding it as utterly new and unique, in having the mind open and wholly receptive.

ALAN WATTS, BRITISH PHILOSOPHER

As we may miss the joy of life by dwelling on the past, so we miss the possibilities of the present if we expect life's best days to be in the future. The good days are now.

LIONEL A. WHISTON, *ENJOY THE JOURNEY*

Live now, believe me, wait not till tomorrow;
Gather the roses of life today.

PIERRE DE RONSARD, FRENCH POET

We're here to feel the joy of life pulsing in us—now.

JOYCE CAROL OATES, AMERICAN WRITER

We cannot put off living until we are ready. The most salient characteristic of life is its urgency 'here and now' without any possible postponement. Life is fired at us point-blank.

JOSÉ ORTEGA Y GASSET, SPANISH PHILOSOPHER

Before, I always lived in anticipation...that it was
all a preparation for something else, something "greater,"
more "genuine." But that feeling has dropped away from
me completely. I live here and now, this minute, this day,
to the full, and the life is worth living.

ELLY HILLESUM, DUTCH DIARIST

One day at a time—this is enough. Do not look back and grieve
over the past, for it is gone; and do not be troubled about the
future, for it has not yet come. Live in the present, and
make it so beautiful it will be worth remembering.

IDA SCOTT TAYLOR, AMERICAN HYMNIST

When you stop comparing what is right here and now with
what you wish were, you can begin to enjoy what is.

CHERI HUBER, AMERICAN ZEN TEACHER

The aim of life is to live, and to live means to be aware,
joyously, drunkenly, serenely, divinely aware.

HENRY MILLER, AMERICAN WRITER

We can enjoy this journey by consciously slowing ourselves
down to live the moment in front of us. We find energy,
joy, humor and grace in that moment. We need to let go
of yesterdays and not be planning tomorrows
but truly savor each present moment.

ANNE BRYAN SMOLLIN, AUTHOR OF *TICKLE YOUR SOUL*

Be intent upon the perfection of the present day.

WILLIAM LAW, BRITISH THEOLOGIAN

I am alive today by the grace of a higher being.
Every day is extra.

JOHN KERRY, AMERICAN POLITICIAN

Life, we learn too late, is in the living,
in the tissue of every day and hour.

STEPHEN LEACOCK, BRITISH-CANADIAN WRITER

I have learned to live each day as it comes,
and not to borrow trouble by dreading tomorrow.

DOROTHY DIX, *HER BOOK*

One must never lose time in vainly regretting the past nor in complaining about the changes which cause us discomfort, for change is the very essence of life.

ANATOLE FRANCE, FRENCH WRITER

Life is all memory, except for the one present moment that goes by you so quickly you hardly catch it going.

TENNESSEE WILLIAMS, AMERICAN PLAYWRIGHT

Life is but a day at most.

ROBERT BURNS, SCOTTISH POET

The golden moments in the stream of life rush past us and we see nothing but sand; the angels come to visit us, and we only know them when they are gone.

GEORGE ELLIOT, BRITISH WRITER

Learn lessons and live in the moment knowing you are mortal. And when in doubt ask: "What would Lassie do?"

BERNIE S. SIEGEL, AUTHOR OF LOVE, MEDICINE AND MIRACLES

You don't get to choose how you're going to die. Or when.
You can only decide how you're going to live. Now.

JOAN BAEZ, AMERICAN FOLK SINGER

Look to this Day!
For it is Life, the very Life of Life.

KALIDASA, INDIAN POET

Keep It Simple

Expect nothing, live frugally on surprise.

ALICE WALKER, AFRICAN-AMERICAN WRITER

If my heart can become pure and simple like that of a child, I think there probably can be no greater happiness than this.

KITARO NISHIDA, BUDDHIST PHILOSOPHER

When I look back over the years, what stands out to me isn't the movies or the games of chess or checkers that I played with my daughter, it's the short trips we took here and there, what we said, and how we felt or the songs we listened to during those brief rides. Enjoy the little journeys; make them the rides your life.

JEFF DAVIDSON, AUTHOR OF *THE JOY OF SIMPLE LIVING*

 Each small task of everyday is part of the total harmony of the universe.

THERESA OF LISIEUX, ROMAN CATHOLIC SAINT

Life is denied by lack of attention, whether it be to cleaning windows or trying to write a masterpiece.

NADIA BOULANGER, FRENCH COMPOSER

The meaning of life is to see.

HUI-NÊNG, CHINESE SAGE

The whole of life lies in the verb seeing.

PIERRE TEILHARD DE CHARDIN, FRENCH JESUIT PRIEST

Look. This is your world! You can't not look. There is no other world. This is your world; it is your feast. You inherited this; you inherited these eyeballs; you inherited this world of color. Look at the greatness of the whole thing. Look! Don't hesitate—look! Open your eyes. Don't blink, and look, look—look further.

CHÔGYAM TRUNGPA, BUDDHIST TEACHER

To be alive, to be able to see, to walk...it's all a miracle.

ARTHUR RUBINSTEIN, POLISH-AMERICAN PIANIST

Life is a great bundle of little things.

OLIVER WENDELL HOLMES, JR., AMERICAN JURIST

One awakens, one rises, one dresses, and one goes forth; One returns, one dines, one sups, one retires and one sleeps.

ANTOINE-PIERRE-AUGUSTIN DE PIIS, FRENCH WRITER

The best things in life are nearest: Breath in your nostrils, light in your eyes, flowers at your feet, duties at your hand, the path of right just before you. Then do not grasp at the stars, but do life's plain, common work as it comes, certain that daily duties and daily bread are the sweetest things in life.

ROBERT LOUIS STEVENSON, SCOTTISH NOVELIST

I'm not going to have a better day, a more magical moment, than the first time I heard my daughter giggle.

SEAN PENN, AMERICAN ACTOR

Life is a child playing around your feet,
a tool you hold firmly in your grip, a bench you
sit down upon in the evening, in your garden.

JEAN ANOUILH, *ANTIGONE*

Ah, the smell of flowers. I've just put flowers in a vase.
The meaning of life is the flowers in a vase.

HELEN CALDICOTT, AUSTRALIAN PHYSICIAN

Just living is enough...one must have sunshine,
freedom, and a little flower.

HANS CHRISTIAN ANDERSEN, DANISH WRITER

If we could see the miracle of a single flower clearly,
our whole life would change.

BUDDHA

We've all had these moments when the heart swells and we feel wordlessly connected to a larger source of loving-kindness and compassion: the times when we surrender to the majesty of a sunset, the caress of a breeze, the laughter of a child, the eyes of a loved one, and we know that life is complete just as it is.

JOAN BORYSENKO, AMERICAN PSYCHOLOGIST

What is life? It is the flash of a firefly in the night. It is the breath of a buffalo in the wintertime. It is the little shadow which runs across the grass and loses itself in the sunset.

CROWFOOT, CANADIAN INDIAN

Be glad of life because it gives you the chance to love and to work and to play and to look up at the stars.

HENRY VAN DYKE, AMERICAN WRITER

Life moves pretty fast. You don't stop and look around once in a while, you could miss it.

MATTHEW BRODERICK IN *FERRIS BUELLER'S DAY OFF*

Good friends, good books and a sleepy conscience: this is the ideal life.

MARK TWAIN, AMERICAN WRITER

When you stop comparing what is right here and now with what you wish were, you can begin to enjoy what is.

CHERI HUBER, AMERICAN ZEN TEACHER

We always have enough to be happy if we are enjoying what we do have—and not worrying about what we don't have.

KEN KEYES, JR., *HANDBOOK TO HIGHER CONSCIOUSNESS*

I finally understand what life is about; it is about losing everything...so every morning we must celebrate what we have.

ISABELLE ALLENDE, PERUVIAN-BORN CHILEAN WRITER

Often people attempt to live their lives backwards; they try to have more things, or more money, in order to do more of what they want, so they will be happier. The way it actually works is the reverse. You must first be who you really are, then do what you need to do, in order to have what you want.

MARGARET YOUNG, AMERICAN SINGER

There must be more to life than having everything!

MAURICE SENDAK, *HIGGLETY PIGGLETY POP!*

When you have only two pennies left in the world,
buy a loaf of bread with one, and a lily with the other.

CHINESE PROVERB

You're only here for a short visit. Don't hurry. Don't worry.
And be sure to smell the flowers along the way.

WALTER HAGEN, AMERICAN GOLFER

If we have a patient mind, all things will unfold in
a natural and organic way. Patience means staying in a
state of balance regardless of what is happening,
staying easy and relaxed and alert.

JOSEPH GOLDSTEIN, *THE EXPERIENCE OF INSIGHT*

The great secret of life...[is] not to open your letters for a
fortnight. At the expiration of that period you will find that
nearly all of them have answered themselves.

ARTHUR BINSTEAD, BRITISH JOURNALIST

**Life just is. You have to flow with it.
Give yourself to the moment. Let it happen.**

JERRY BROWN, AMERICAN POLITICIAN

**Just chill out and reproduce.
Keep the species alive.**

ICE-T, AMERICAN RAP ARTIST

**I have a simple philosophy.
Fill what's empty. Empty what's full.
And scratch where it itches.**

ALICE ROOSEVELT LONGWORTH, DAUGHTER OF
U.S. PRESIDENT THEODORE ROOSEVELT

**Struggle mightily until you realize that you are
everything and there is no need to struggle.**

DALE BORGLUM, AMERICAN THANATOLOGIST

Create the Life You Like

Each of us is given a bit of the raw material of life with which to work. We can shape it any way we wish. The time in which we live, our inheritance of traits, etc., all have something to do with what we become, but after that it is in our hands to do much with what we have. Physically and mentally we can shape it any way we desire.

LOUIS L'AMOUR, AMERICAN WRITER

Our lives are like an exploding sky rocket—the kind you might use in a 4th of July nighttime fireworks display. Inside the rocket are elements that burst into brilliant, cascading colors, illuminating the darkness, attracting the "oohs" and "ahs" of people. Like the rocket you have something inside you, that's there to get out, to explode.

CY EBERHART, AMERICAN CLERGYMAN

When you discover your mission, you will feel its demand. It will fill you with enthusiasm and a burning desire to get to work on it.

W. CLEMENT STONE, AMERICAN BUSINESSMAN

When you are working towards fulfilling your true purpose you discover astonishing gifts within yourself that you may have never known you have.

CHÉRIE CARTER-SCOTT, *IF LIFE IS A GAME, THESE ARE THE RULES*

Figure out what makes you tick and go with it. If you do, life will be blissful. If you try to go against it, the universe will give you a swift kick in the pants.

ED BRODOW, AUTHOR OF *BEATING THE SUCCESS TRAP*

If you follow your bliss, you put yourself on a kind of track that has been there all the while, waiting for you, and the life that you ought to be living.

JOSEPH CAMPBELL, *THE POWER OF MYTH*

You nourish your soul by fulfilling your destiny.

HAROLD S. KUSHNER, AUTHOR OF *WHEN BAD THINGS HAPPEN TO GOOD PEOPLE*

You have to take it as it happens, but you should try
to make it happen the way you want to take it.

GERMAN PROVERB

The value of life lies not in the length of days
but in the use you make of them.

MICHEL DE MONTAIGNE, FRENCH ESSAYIST

The greatest use of life is to spend it for
something that will outlast it.

WILLIAM JAMES, AMERICAN PSYCHOLOGIST

Every man has a mandate
to fill the contours of his being.

GUY DAVENPORT, TATLIN

Acting as if you were already what you want to become and
knowing that you can become it is the way to remove
self-doubt and enter your real-magic kingdom.

WAYNE DYER, EVERYDAY WISDOM

Don't wait for extraordinary opportunities.
Seize common occasions and make them great.

ORISON SWETT MARDEN, FOUNDER OF *SUCCESS MAGAZINE*

Too many of us consent, or are forced, to spend time doing things for which we have no heartfelt reason.... We do it to hold a job, to make a living, to satisfy the expectations of others, to fill our time, to evade the fact that we don't know what else to do—but not because the doing comes from inside us. When our action is dictated by factors external to our soul, we do not live active lives but reactive lives.

PARKER J. PALMER, *THE ACTIVE LIFE*

Your work is going to fill a large part of your life, and the only way to be truly satisfied is to do what you believe is great work. And the only way to do great work is to love what you do. If you haven't found it yet, keep looking. Don't settle.

STEVE JOBS, FOUNDER OF APPLE COMPUTER

Lives, like money, are spent.
What are you buying with yours?

ROY H. WILLIAMS, AMERICAN COLUMNIST

You can't hit a home run unless you step up to the plate.
You can't catch fish unless you put your line in the water.
You can't reach your goals if you don't try.

KATHY SELIGMAN, AMERICAN JOURNALIST

All the answers you are looking for are already within your
grasp: all you need to do is look inside, listen, and trust
yourself. There is no outside source of wisdom that can
give you the answers to any of your innermost questions;
you alone are your wisest teacher. Deep inside,
you already know all you need to know.

CHÉRIE CARTER-SCOTT, *IF LIFE IS A GAME, THESE ARE THE RULES*

Two agendas are prevalent in your life: Heaven's and yours.
Often these two will clash with each other. When what we want
our lives to be is different from our intended destiny, the uni-
versal will creates roadblocks.

CHIN-NING CHU, *DO LESS, ACHIEVE MORE*

If we are facing in the right direction,
all we have to do is keep on walking.

BUDDHIST PROVERB

Each person on this planet is inherently, intrinsically capable of attaining "dizzying heights" of happiness and fulfillment.

WAYNE DYER, *THE SKY'S THE LIMIT*

**What a wonderful life I've had!
I only wish I'd realized it sooner.**

COLETTE, FRENCH WRITER

**There is only one success—to be able
to spend your life in your own way.**

CHRISTOPHER MORLEY, AMERICAN NOVELIST

**God asks no man whether he will accept life. That is not the
choice. One must take it. The only choice is how.**

HENRY WARD BEECHER, AMERICAN CLERGYMAN

Life will have just as much meaning for you as you put into it.

WILL DURANT, AMERICAN PHILOSOPHER

**If life doesn't offer a game worth playing,
then invent a new one.**

ANTHONY J. D'ANGELO, *THE COLLEGE BLUE BOOK*

**And life is what we make it.
Always has been, always will be.**

GRANDMA MOSES, AMERICAN ARTIST

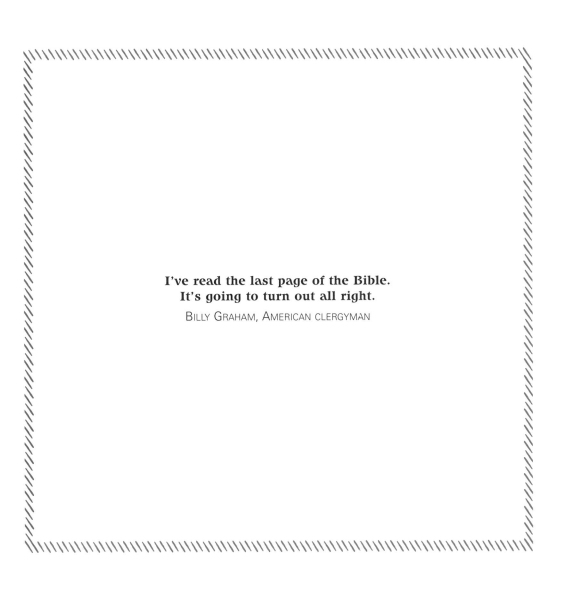

**I've read the last page of the Bible.
It's going to turn out all right.**

BILLY GRAHAM, AMERICAN CLERGYMAN

Index to Authors

D

E

F

ABOUT THE AUTHOR

Allen Klein is an award-winning professional speaker, best-selling author, and the President of the Association for Applied and Therapeutic Humor (www.aath.org). He teaches people worldwide how to use humor to deal with not-so-funny stuff. In addition to this book, Klein is also the author of *Up Words for Down Days, The Change-Your-Life Quote Book, The Lift-Your-Spirits Quote Book, The Celebrate-Your-Life Quote Book, The Simplify-Your-Life Book, The Love and Kisses Quote Book* and *The Wise and Witty Quote Book,* among others.

For more information about Klein or his presentations go to www.allenklein.com, or e-mail him at humor@allenklein.com